GOD
OF
SURPRISE

GOD
OF
SURPRISE

THE LIFE-CHANGING,
UNEXPECTED WAYS
GOD WORKS FOR OUR GOOD

BILL
CROWDER

Our Daily Bread
Publishing™

Requests for permission to quote from this book should be directed to:
Permissions Department, Our Daily Bread Publishing, PO Box 3566, Grand
Rapids, MI 49501, or contact us by email at permissionsdept@odb.org.

Scripture quotations, unless otherwise indicated, are from the New American Standard Bible®, Copyright © 1960, 1962, 1963, 1968, 1971, 1973, 1977, 1995 by The Lockman Foundation. Used by permission. (Lockman.org)

Scripture quotations marked MEV are from The Holy Bible, Modern English Version. Copyright © 2014 by Military Bible Association. Published and distributed by Charisma House. All rights reserved.

Scripture quotations marked NKJV are from the New King James Version®. Copyright © 1982 by Thomas Nelson. Used by permission.

Interior design by Sam Carbaugh

Library of Congress Cataloging-in-Publication Data

Names: Crowder, Bill, author.
Title: God of surprise : the life-changing, unexpected ways God works for
  our good / Bill Crowder.
Description: Grand Rapids, Michigan : Our Daily Bread Publishing, 2020.
  | Summary: "Find a new sense of hope as you witness the mysterious and
  thoroughly unpredictable ways God intervened in the experiences of men
  and women in the Bible"-- Provided by publisher.
Identifiers: LCCN 2019046720 (print) | LCCN 2019046721 (ebook) | ISBN
  9781640700086 (paperback) | ISBN 9781640700611 (ebook)
Subjects: LCSH: God (Christianity)--Goodness. | Providence and government of God--Christianity. | God (Christianity)--Goodness--Biblical
  teaching. | Providence and government of God--Christianity--Biblical
  teaching.
Classification: LCC BT137 .C76 2020 (print) | LCC BT137 (ebook) |
  DDC 231.7/6--dc23
LC record available at https://lccn.loc.gov/2019046720
LC ebook record available at https://lccn.loc.gov/2019046721

Printed in the United States of America

20 21 22 23 24 25 26 27 / 8 7 6 5 4 3 2 1

For teachers who have made a difference in my life:

Tobyann Davis, who taught me how to speak.
Ed Dobson, who taught me how to persevere.
Earl Miller, who taught me how teach and preach.
Mike Wilkins, who taught me how to think.

I am deeply grateful.

Contents

Acknowledgments

Haddon Robinson, the great teacher of preachers, liked to say, "If you see a turtle on a fence post, you know one thing for sure—it didn't get there by itself."

While I am convinced that the evidence of life clearly bears this out, I feel the weight of it particularly in the process of bringing a book to life. In some ways the writing process is isolating—but that is only part of the greater whole. The number of hands, hearts, and minds that are applied to taking a piece like this from its concept to the finished presentation is enormous. In the end, the isolated work of writing feeds into a process that is highly collaborative and, thankfully for me, deeply collegial. To produce a book, you don't get there by yourself.

As a result, whenever I have the privilege of trying to capture thoughts on a page, I do so knowing I am not on a fence post—I am a part of teams that help bring about a book that will, we trust, strengthen men and women in their walk with Christ.

The editorial team at Our Daily Bread Publishing has encouraged me and evaluated the ideas, polished the prose, and pursued excellence in every facet of this book. I am grateful for each of my friends there. Ken Peterson, the publisher, and Miranda Gardner, the former executive editor, were tremendously helpful in refining ideas and thinking through the most helpful ways to present them to our readers. The acquisitions committee of Dave Branon, Meaghan Minkus, Dawn Anderson, and Mike Nappa helped polish the approach and accepted the proposal. Dave himself worked tirelessly to help edit and strengthen the material so it would be as accessible as possible to you.

Our Daily Bread Publishing's marketing team—John van der Veen, Cathy Sall, and Marjie Johnson—worked hard to assure that all of this work would eventually end up in your hands. I have said it before, but it never gets old: It is a privilege to work not just with a team but with a team of friends.

My ultimate teammate and best friend, however, is my wife Marlene. Over the years, she has been my most trusted sounding board, most consistent encourager, and most loving critic. I continually give thanks that my good, good Father brought her into my life. Our kids and grandkids support me with a level of encouragement that helps me move forward when the isolated part of writing gets long and hard. My family is another team—and a wonderful gift from God.

On the dedication page, I mentioned four teachers from my Bible college and seminary days who had a lasting impact on my life. I could have listed many more, but these four are representative of many others who invested in my future ministry many decades ago. Their contributions in my life remain an enduring gift for which I am thankful.

And even in the lonely parts of the writing process, I am never alone. The surprising God we explore together in these pages is also the wonderfully trustworthy and utterly faithful One who has promised He will never leave us or forsake us (Hebrews 13:5). No matter how surprising He might be, His presence is life's greatest reality. Thanks for joining me for this journey of discovering Him together.

Introduction

But God . . .

In the film version of C. S. Lewis's classic fantasy *The Chronicles of Narnia: The Lion, the Witch and the Wardrobe*, a fascinating scene occurs as Aslan—the mighty lion that pictures Christ—is walking away from a celebration in Narnia's palace. Lucy Pevensee, a young girl miraculously transported into Narnia, is standing with her friend Mr. Tumnus, the fawn. As they watch Aslan depart, she wonders aloud about Aslan and when they might see him again. Mr. Tumnus responds, "You mustn't press him, he isn't a tame lion." Lucy's response? "No, but he's good."

This is part of what makes God mysterious to us. He is not a tame lion. He is absolutely dependable yet thoroughly unpredictable. We can trust His character, but His ways can be difficult to understand. This paradoxical reality was perfectly captured by Isaiah the prophet, who wrote:

> "For My thoughts are not your thoughts, nor are your ways My ways," declares the LORD. "For as the heavens are higher than the earth, so are My ways higher than your ways and My thoughts than your thoughts." (Isaiah 55:8–9)

In recent years, I have found great comfort in those words. Many people question what God is doing when our world—whether globally or privately—seems to be unraveling. The frustrations and struggles we encounter can be amplified when our questions find no answers.

The unpredictability of God, however, does not need to be threatening or fear-inducing. Instead, it can be a reminder of a wisdom that is eternal, in contrast to ours, which is time-bound. It can be a reminder of purposes that are flawless and perfect, while our desires are often fleeting and self-absorbed. Yes, He is the God who often surprises us with His ways—but that is actually *good* news.

This good news of our surprising God is often reflected throughout the Scriptures with the little phrase, "But God . . ." This expression is found more than forty times in the Bible. While many of those instances reflect the narrative story line, some show the surprising ways God intervenes in the experiences of men and women—both then and now.

In order to wrestle with God's mysterious workings, in this book we will consider in detail six of those "But God . . ." moments. In those surprising, unpredictable interventions, we can see how God turns life on its ear while accomplishing His wonderful purposes. We can see how our wise God sometimes surprises us with His wisdom. And we can see how our God's designs can be both surprisingly counterintuitive and deeply comforting.

The Surprise of Divine Rescue

Perhaps for a good man some would even dare to die. ***But God*** *demonstrates His own love toward us, in that while we were yet sinners, Christ died for us.*

ROMANS 5:7–8 (MEV)

The Wild Boars were in serious trouble.

The Thai youth soccer team was trapped by rising waters in a cave in Thailand, and the world was holding its collective breath. Twelve young boys, ranging in age from eleven to seventeen, and their coach had entered the cave for a brief time of exploration, but no one could have imagined the near-death experience this seemingly innocent visit would become. A sudden rainstorm flooded the cave and cut off the team's escape. Without food or clean water, all seemed lost in the treacherous caves that sank to a depth of some ten miles below the earth's surface.

The Thai military immediately began a search-and-rescue operation, but it would take nine days to locate the team and six more days before the final boy was pulled from danger.

The rescue was expensive—one of the Thai rescuers, a former Thai Navy SEAL, lost his life during the attempt—but social media erupted with celebration as the ordeal had a happy ending. Mission accomplished.

It seems to be an ever-present part of the modern news cycle—tragedy begets crisis, which in turn begets rescue.

A sailor lost at sea.

A missing child.

An abused spouse.

A group of coworkers taken hostage.

A hiker trapped.

In each case, every second is precious as the risk of loss intensifies. And in each case, every second is clouded by concern that the rescue would come too late and that eventually the search-and-rescue mission might dissolve into a search-and-recovery operation.

What I find interesting is that in the realm of human rescue, no one asks whether the trapped child or drowning seaman or abused wife *deserves* to be rescued. No one asks about the person's political affiliation, family pedigree, or religious background. The desperate reality of the situation supersedes any such thought of whether or not rescue is deserved—it is a given that all means available will be used to secure the rescue of the endangered persons.

Yet we who have been rescued by our Savior, Jesus Christ, often seem to deal with people outside of the family of God in terms of deserving and underserving instead of merely seeing them in terms of their deep, desperate, eternal need.

This is why God's rescue of the undeserving seems so surprising. So unexpected. Paul describes our rescue, and the little phrase "But God . . ." is at the heart of the surprise:

> And you were dead in your trespasses and sins, in which you formerly walked according to the course of this world, according to the prince of the power of the air, of the spirit that is now working in the sons of disobedience. Among them we too all formerly lived in the lusts of our flesh, indulging the desires of the flesh and of the mind, and were by nature children of wrath, even as the rest. **But God,** being rich in mercy, because of His great love with which He loved us, even when we were dead in our transgressions, made us alive together with Christ (by grace you have been saved), and raised us up with Him, and seated us with Him in the heavenly places in Christ Jesus, so that in the ages to come He might show the surpassing riches of His grace in kindness toward us in Christ Jesus. (Ephesians 2:1–7)

Our Desperate Situation

I have often joked that minor surgery is when an operation is performed on someone else. If, however, they are cutting on me, it's major. No matter how insignificant the procedure might be deemed. Perhaps that is why I still have my tonsils and my appendix. Perhaps that explains why I have never . . . ever . . .

gone under the knife. It is one thing when other people are undergoing operations—everything feels much, much different when we are on the table.

This is a valuable perspective check. When we look at those outside Christ and try to determine whether they do or do not deserve Christ's rescue, we can easily evaluate them with a different standard than we would apply to ourselves. We tend to consider any number of items—lifestyle choices, gender identity, politics, ethnicity, nationality, or a thousand other things. For many of us, we watch in horror as terrorists behead westerners on YouTube—and we demand that they be brought to justice. Similarly, we read news reports of pedophiles who sexually exploit and abuse young, vulnerable children; and we cry out for their imprisonment.

We know that we didn't deserve mercy, but somehow we view them differently. They *really* don't deserve mercy. They deserve punishment. But while justice may call for judgment temporally, what about eternally? Do we pray for their spiritual rescue as passionately as we scream for their present-tense judgment? Maybe not—because anyone who would do *that* doesn't deserve rescue. It makes perfect sense to us. But that is the opposite of God's perspective. He fully and clearly sees the depth of our lostness and the darkness of our sin. He fully understands that all of us deserve to bear the full weight of our wrongs—and He sent Jesus to our rescue anyway.

Talk about counterintuitive! The "But God . . ." of rescue is shocking when we compare our undeservedness to the overwhelming price that our rescue would cost. How desperate

was our situation? Hear again Paul's inspired assessment of
the human condition:

> And you were dead in your trespasses and sins, in
> which you formerly walked according to the course
> of this world, according to the prince of the power of
> the air, of the spirit that is now working in the sons of
> disobedience. Among them we too all formerly lived
> in the lusts of our flesh, indulging the desires of the
> flesh and of the mind, and were by nature children
> of wrath, even as the rest. (Ephesians 2:1–3)

While Paul addressed his Ephesian readers with the
word *you*, I want us to make it just as personal as possible
to us. These words clearly portray the condition of each of
us—apart from Christ.

"Dead in trespasses and sins" Lost.
"Walked according to the course of this world" Broken.
"According to the prince of the power of the air" Hopeless.
"Sons of disobedience" Undeserving.

And these descriptors aren't simply being applied to
"those" people "out there." Paul joins his name to the Ephesian
Christ-followers saying, "We too." All of us come from the
same tragic place. And that is what makes the "But God . . ."
moment so spectacular. He dared to do what seemed to be the
most unthinkable for the most undeserving—which includes
every last one of us.

God's Daring Rescue Mission

In the closing days of the Pacific Campaign of World War II, intelligence reports in the Philippines revealed that Allied prisoners of war and civilian collaborators were being summarily executed. This created a dire situation for the more than five hundred men being held at the Cabanatuan prison camp about seventy miles north of Manila—they were living their last days.

So, the Filipino militia and American troops joined together to engage in a bold plan to rescue those prisoners before they could be killed. On January 30, 1945, Lt. Col. Henry Mucci led his Army Rangers and Filipino resistance fighters in an assault on the camp that would result in two Allied casualties—yet that sacrifice and the courageous mission would secure the rescue of the doomed prisoners.

To this day, the rescue mission is referred to as "The Great Raid" (made popular in a film by the same name). But why was the raid undertaken? Why risk so many lives in order to rescue those prisoners of war? The answer to that question seems self-evident. It is the same reason we move heaven and earth to rescue trapped miners or kidnapped children or abused wives or captured hostages. In our deepest hearts, we understand that a human being is worth something.

For followers of Christ, the worth of a person is deeply rooted in the Scriptures—we are called to see human beings as image-bearers of God. They are eternal souls with eternal worth and eternal value. When we see that, we are seeing what our God sees. In the face of the brokenness of the human condition that we just considered in Ephesians 2:1–3, God, who perfectly understands how woeful and wayward we are, nevertheless launched a rescue mission of global proportions, and He launched it at the greatest of costs. Paul continues:

> **But God,** being rich in mercy, because of His great love with which He loved us, even when we were dead in sins, made us alive together with Christ (by grace you have been saved), and He raised us up and seated us together in the heavenly places in Christ Jesus, so that in the coming ages He might show the surpassing riches of His grace in kindness toward us in Christ Jesus. (Ephesians 2:4–7 MEV)

I love that. One of the first things I heard as a new follower of Jesus was that although I deserved justice, He gave me mercy. That is where the rescue mission began—in the mercy of God. And notice that not only is God a God of mercy but Paul affirms that He is also "rich in mercy." That explains the extravagant lengths to which the Creator went to secure our rescue.

Even more, the "But God" piece of the statement sets His mercy in contrast—not to our lack of mercy but to the reality that we could never deserve that mercy. The "But God" is a statement of shock and awe. It is an amazed, slack-jawed reminder of the fact that His mercy is not for the deserving. No one is in that category. His mercy is in full awareness of the fact that mercy is given—not earned.

How did God deploy that mercy on behalf of the undeserving? In the Christ. Through Jesus, our God lavishes upon us unexpected, extravagant mercy so that, rolling over us like a tsunami of compassion, we receive life in Christ and a place in the Father's house (see also John 14:1–4). Why did He do this? At least part of the answer is found in Ephesians 2:7: "so that in the ages to come He might show the surpassing riches of His grace in *kindness* toward us in Christ Jesus" (emphasis added).

This divine, unimaginable kindness found its fullest expression in the person of Jesus:

> But when the *kindness* of God our Savior and His love for mankind appeared, He saved us, not on the basis of deeds which we have done in righteousness, but according to His mercy, by the washing of regeneration and renewing by the Holy Spirit, whom He poured out upon us richly through Jesus Christ our Savior. (Titus 3:4–6; emphasis added)

And this kindness that reveals the "surpassing riches of His grace" (Ephesians 2:7) and sent Jesus to our rescue leads us to repentance:

> Or do you think lightly of the riches of His kindness and tolerance and patience, not knowing that the *kindness* of God leads you to repentance? (Romans 2:4; emphasis added)

God's daring kindness is the driving force behind the surpassing riches of His grace and mercy. And this kindness found its full force in the rescue that we have received in Christ.

Rescue's Amazing Motive

Is it possible that high-powered, high-volume television infomercials are the ultimate bane of the modern world? People hawking their products by proclaiming passionately that your life will be desperately diminished if you don't buy their gadget—whatever it is. Then, just when you think they can't press any harder, you hear those enticing words, "But wait! There's more!" More? Yes, but only if you call in the next fifteen minutes. More.

While those words feel strangely empty when coming from a spokesperson in a slickly produced TV ad, there is nothing empty about the reality of *more* in God's motives for our rescue. We have seen that this rescue was driven by kindness and fueled by mercy. But in fact there *is* more. Paul wraps up all of these important ideas in his letter to the Romans—and once again our now-anticipated, wonderfully welcome "But God" is at the heart of it all.

For while we were still helpless, at the right time Christ died for the ungodly. For one will hardly die for a righteous man; though perhaps for the good man someone would dare even to die. **But God** demonstrates His own love toward us, in that while we were yet sinners, Christ died for us. (Romans 5:6–8)

Notice again that Paul doesn't dodge the monumental, insurmountable problem we face. Not only does he face the problem of sin head-on but the apostle also describes the reality of that problem—finding someone to sacrifice himself for us. For a good person, maybe—although Paul has already conclusively proven that there is none that does good, not even one (Romans 3:10). But for us? All of whom are guilty as charged? Not a chance.

This takes us back to where we began in this chapter. The deserving versus the undeserving. The good enough versus the too bad. The in versus the out.

But God . . .

We can be eternally grateful that our God is not driven by what we deserve or don't deserve, nor is He compelled by our ability to get there under our own steam. This is the more. Not only is God driven by kindness and moved by mercy but He is also ultimately motived by His love.

I have friends who see the cross as the solution to God's wrath. They are convinced that God's anger against us for our sin was so intense and so insatiable that it could only be resolved by the death of Christ on the cross. Perhaps they are correct, and I know many good theologians who hold to that view.

But for me there is *more*. When I read the most famous verse in the Bible, I see a different satisfaction—and it lines up completely with what we are seeing in Romans 5:8: "For

God *so loved* the world, that He gave His only begotten Son, that whoever believes in Him shall not perish, but have eternal life." (John 3:16; emphasis added)

I can't get past the "so loved." Especially the "so." It was God's love that provided the cross. Why? Because His love could be satisfied no other way. This is what Paul is telling us in Romans 5 as well. God has proven His *love* toward us. How? By having Christ die for us when we were the most unworthy. The most undeserving. The most guilty.

This is the great surprise of God's rescue—it is not the response of righteous anger to our sin or the deliberate reward for religious deeds, but it is the declaration that His holy love is greater than our worst selves.

My Personal "But God" Moment

I grew up going to church, but to be candid, it was not a church where I can ever remember hearing the message of the cross clearly presented. I remember as a boy hearing the occasional television message when Billy Graham talked about the cross, and I remember being invited by a friend to a church that was hosting a visiting evangelist. But during most of my growing up years, I experienced church as ritual. What was there was not terrible. However, what was missing was enormous.

I finished high school, quit college, and like many of my generation, followed many of the troubling trends of the '60s in both lifestyle and attitude. I was not simply aimless or misguided, I was lost. Well and truly lost.

As a young adult, I was hospitalized as a result of a work-related accident. I fell thirty-eight feet off a railroad bridge and was hospitalized with a sprained neck. I was the talk of the hospital. As I lay in my bed immobilized in traction, I could hear people stopping at the door of my room to speculate about how I had survived that devastating fall, which should have been fatal. I had gone from being profoundly lost to being little more than a curiosity.

One day, however, I heard my roommate and his wife softly crying. I couldn't see them because my head and neck were held fast by the traction device. But I could tell that they were elderly, and I assumed their weeping meant they had received bad news from their doctor. I couldn't have been more wrong. They were crying for me.

When the man's wife began to leave at the end of visiting hours, she detoured to my bed and leaned over to look deeply into my eyes—her eyes still glistening with tears. She explained that they had been discussing my accident and had committed themselves to praying for me. They were followers of Christ and believed that God had spared my life for a reason.

This was new information for me. I had no idea that God was even really there, let alone that He had any interest in me. It was a brief moment in a hospital room, yet it set my feet on a path to God and the rescue He has provided in Christ. God cared for me. And no one knew better than I did how undeserving I was.

But God did more than just care about me. He loved me so much that He sacrificed His one and only Son to bring me home. As a follower of Jesus, I have come to understand that every testimony of faith in Christ is another deeply personal, extremely intimate "But God" event. The rescue that His mercy and kindness and love orchestrated altered my personal direction from utter lostness to undeserved rescue.

Believe me. I know what I am and I know what I was. And I know that there is only one explanation—the love of God interrupting my self-destruction with life and hope and mercy. I marvel at that. And I trust that if you have met the Savior, you marvel at your personal "But God" experience as well. Undoubtedly it is this sense of wonder that prompted hymnwriter Charles Gabriel to marvel:

I stand amazed in the presence
of Jesus, the Nazarene,
and wonder how He could love me,
a sinner, condemned, unclean.
How marvelous! How wonderful!
And my song shall ever be:
How marvelous, how wonderful
is my Savior's love for me!

But God. The rescuing God whose love, kindness, and mercy all reach to us in Jesus. How marvelous! How wonderful!

Rescuing Father, I know who I am. I know what I am. And I know how undeserving I am of your costly, priceless rescue. In the moments of life when pain visits my experience or hardships tax my heart, remind me that your love is not defined by my circumstances or struggles, but by your willingness to send Jesus to provide for my forgiveness and restore me to relationship with you. Thank you, Father, for your powerful, perfect love, mercy, and kindness. I am thankful.

Chapter Two

The Surprise
of Life Out of Death

This Man, delivered over by the predetermined
plan and foreknowledge of God, you nailed
to a cross by the hands of godless men and put
Him to death. **But God** *raised Him up again,*
putting an end to the agony of death, since it
was impossible for Him to be held in its power.

Acts 2:23–24

I had been a pastor for three days when I performed my first funeral. It was the memorial service for my father, William Earl Crowder, for whom I was named. Although those long days after my father's death were filled with darkness and loss, it was an event that revealed to me in absolute, high-definition clarity that despite my years of study in Bible college, my semesters as a teacher at that same Bible college, and countless opportunities for itinerant preaching, I was largely unprepared for what awaited me as a pastor.

The job was just too big for me.

But I also learned something else that painted a picture with a much broader context. For the first time, I discovered that in our culture and in our day we do whatever we can to avoid the subject of death. And usually it is at funerals, memorial services, or celebrations of life (or whatever the current phrase of comfort may be) that we are dragged, kicking and screaming, to a moment where we must come face-to-face with death.

In spite of our modern aversion to the subject, however, we apparently have a deep need to talk about death. Others have already joined this important conversation, offering perspectives ranging from the philosophical to the humorous:

Musician Bob Dylan sang, "He not busy bein' born is busy dyin'."

Filmmaker Woody Allen opined, "I'm not afraid to die. I just don't want to be there when it happens."

Statesman Winston Churchill offered, "I am prepared to meet my Maker. Whether my Maker is prepared for the great ordeal of meeting me is another matter."

Comedian Groucho Marx joked, "I intend to live forever, or die trying."

Yes, what we can't avoid we attempt to dilute with humor. But there is more. A surprising, deeply serious perspective on death was offered by the late Steve Jobs as he battled pancreatic cancer. The cofounder of Apple and the creative genius behind the tech firm's amazing success said:

No one wants to die. Even people who want to go to heaven don't want to die to get there. And yet death is the destination we all share. No one has ever escaped it. And that is as it should be, because Death is very likely the single best invention of Life. It is Life's change agent. It clears out the old to make way for the new.

Rose Kennedy (mother of John F. Kennedy and Robert Kennedy) viewed death from a deeply personal perspective, saying:

> I tell myself that God gave my children many gifts—spirit, beauty, intelligence, the capacity to make friends and to inspire respect. There was only one gift he held back—length of life.

Death has long threatened us, causing us to battle for the length of life Rose Kennedy felt her children lacked. We wonder how to avoid or forestall our appointment with dying. It is that passion that, according to legend, drove Ponce de Leon to spend his life looking for a fountain of youth. The fictional Indiana Jones and his father searched the deserts of the Middle East for the Holy Grail, believing that it would give the owner eternal life. Modern medical advances extend our years to lengths previously unheard of. We are perpetually pursuing life without death.

Nevertheless, death remains that thing that hangs out there in front of us. The appointment, as one person put it, that none of us can avoid. The inevitable destination at the end of every road. One out of every one still dies.

But for the follower of Christ, though death is filled with mystery, it does not need to be filled with anxiety—because death is not the end. The Death-Conqueror has come and taken the power out of death's hands. And here is the surprise—He conquered death by dying.

So, where do we start in our consideration of death and dying? We go all the way back to the beginning.

When Death Was Born

Consider for a moment our first parents, created as image-bearers of God and placed within an environment of perfect tranquility and full provision. As Adam and Eve enjoyed everything the Creator had made, it would be easy to think that the first thing actually *born* in their newly created realm was Cain, their first son. In reality, however, Cain's birth was preceded by another, more ominous, birth: the birth of death.

Genesis 3 takes us back into that perfect garden of light and life and allows us to witness the collapse that produced death and dying:

> Now the serpent was more crafty than any beast of the field which the LORD God had made. And he said to the woman, "Indeed, has God said, 'You shall not eat from any tree of the garden'?" The woman said to the

serpent, "From the fruit of the trees of the garden we may eat; but from the fruit of the tree which is in the middle of the garden, God has said, 'You shall not eat from it or touch it, or you will die.'" The serpent said to the woman, "You surely will not die! For God knows that in the day you eat from it your eyes will be opened, and you will be like God, knowing good and evil." When the woman saw that the tree was good for food, and that it was a delight to the eyes, and that the tree was desirable to make one wise, she took from its fruit and ate; and she gave also to her husband with her, and he ate. Then the eyes of both of them were opened, and they knew that they were naked; and they sewed fig leaves together and made themselves loin coverings.

They heard the sound of the LORD God walking in the garden in the cool of the day, and the man and his wife hid themselves from the presence of the LORD God among the trees of the garden. Then the LORD God called to the man, and said to him, "Where are you?" He said, "I heard the sound of You in the garden, and I was afraid because I was naked; so I hid myself." (Genesis 3:1–10)

Fear had replaced peace, and distance had replaced relationship. Even more, although it was not yet part of their experience, death had become an inevitable part of life. We can wrestle with the theological mysteries of God's decrees and why there was a dangerous tree in the midst of an otherwise unflawed home for the man and the woman. We could discuss Adam's failure to properly explain God's commands to his wife so she could be prepared for the enemy's subtleties. We could focus on Eve's gullibility and the ease with which she was seduced. Or we could consider the Enemy and his plot to derail God's creative wonders before they had barely even begun to be expressed.

All of those things are important ideas and worthy of consideration, but in the end we still end up in the same place. The creation that a loving, benevolent God had designed to nurture and sustain life would now be invaded by death. What was at the root of that death? A lie rooted in the twisting of God's words of caution. In a world of plenty and fullness, the first couple literally had everything—but they wanted one more thing. They wanted to be like God (v. 4). Not just to bear His image, but rather, to *be* His image.

The recklessness of this desire placed the human race on a path of devolution. Rather than being *like* God, men and women became more and more *unlike* Him. With their hearts spoiled by sin and its destructive consequences, the man and the woman ushered in a stream of human experience that was never what God had intended for His creation. He had given life and all that was needed to sustain it. They had chosen death and all that it does to consume us.

The ultimate global consequence of their fall was the death of all who would come after them. The world God had created as a sanctuary for life had become one vast, unending cemetery as death became the dominant reality in a world once-perfect, now broken. In fact, this broken world and its broken inhabitants would ultimately rise up to bring death upon the Creator who had given them life.

When Death Killed Life

In the film *Meet Joe Black*, Death (portrayed by Brad Pitt) takes up residence in a human body in order to experience life and to understand why humans cling to it so desperately. Along the way, he sees firsthand the wonders of love and the horrors of treachery—and he finds it difficult to let go of the life that he has assumed. In the end, however, filled with new and intimate knowledge of why life is so precious, Death returns to his role as the life-taker. Destroying, not delivering.

Fictional movies and novels can give us a space in which to think about things outside the realms of our experience— but at the end of the day they are just stories that, though blurred reflections of elements of reality, are rooted in imagination—not truth.

In the case of Joe Black, it was not a reflection of the truth that was in view. Instead, it was a photographic negative of the real story. The real story is that Life, not Death, is the One who came to this small planet in human form. And He did not come to experience life but to experience death on behalf of the creation that had rebelled against Him.

The story of Jesus is the truest of true stories. The One who came to give life that would be overflowing and abundant (John 10:10) would be assaulted by His own image-bearers, who would visit death upon the One who is the Life

(John 14:6). Fifty days after the events of Christ's passion, one of his followers, Simon Peter, stood up in the midst of a festival crowd in Jerusalem and declared:

> Men of Israel, listen to these words: Jesus the Nazarene, a man attested to you by God with miracles and wonders and signs which God performed through Him in your midst, just as you yourselves know—this Man, delivered over by the predetermined plan and foreknowledge of God, you nailed to a cross by the hands of godless men and put Him to death. (Acts 2:22–23)

Peter made no attempt to be subtle or nuanced. He was not seeking to be diplomatic or statesmanlike. He confronted the problem head-on—Jesus had come, and the people had killed Him. Make no mistake, it was God's plan and purpose from long ago ("delivered over by the predetermined plan and foreknowledge of God" v. 23), but in no way is the crime of humanity lessened by this fact. The people had witnessed Jesus's power, love, and grace ("as you yourselves know" v. 22). They had seen the undeniable evidence of the Father's affirmation of Jesus's identity ("attested to you by God" v. 22), yet they had joined together, Jew and Gentile alike, to nail God's Son to a cross.

However, even though this act of rebellion and rejection was utterly unthinkable, it was not unanticipated. One of Israel's own ancient prophets had—long before the Savior arrived—warned that when He came He would be rejected:

He was despised and forsaken of men,
A man of sorrows and acquainted with grief;
And like one from whom men hide their face
He was despised, and we did not esteem Him.

Surely our griefs He Himself bore,
And our sorrows He carried;
Yet we ourselves esteemed Him stricken,
Smitten of God, and afflicted.
But He was pierced through for our transgressions,
He was crushed for our iniquities;
The chastening for our well-being fell upon Him,
And by His scourging we are healed.
All of us like sheep have gone astray,
Each of us has turned to his own way;
But the Lord has caused the iniquity of us all
To fall on Him.

(Isaiah 53:3–6)

Our lostness was most clearly evidenced by our clear, unmitigated rejection of the One who had come to rescue us. Like sheep gone astray, we wandered from our God, but like ravenous wolves we sought to destroy Him with hate and violence. And the most shocking thing was this: We decided that He deserved it. "We ourselves esteemed Him stricken, smitten of God, and afflicted" (Isaiah 53:4).

But that was not the full truth of the death of Life. He bore *our* griefs, *our* sorrows, and *our* sins. And He carried them all the way to His own death. He allowed himself to be consumed by all that had consumed us, taking on himself the consequences of wrongs He had not committed and rebellion He had not performed. In our place, Life allowed himself to be killed by death. But, thankfully, Peter's message doesn't end there. It has a victory chorus to sing.

When Life Conquered Death

> "Winning isn't everything; it's the only thing." —Vince Lombardi, Hall of Fame football coach; winner of Super Bowl I and Super Bowl II

> "Some people believe football is a matter of life and death. I am very disappointed with that attitude. I can assure you it is much, much more important than that." —Bill Shankly, legendary manager of Liverpool (England) Football Club

These quotes have motivated me in the past because, I will confess to you, I am very competitive. Maybe it is the result of growing up with three brothers who were vastly superior to me athletically. Whether in basketball, golf, badminton, or even bowling, I was rarely able to beat them—but the competitive juices that those times generated never went away. As a result, when I played goalkeeper on my college's intercollegiate soccer team, I was driven by an almost indescribable hunger for victory. In fact, it is probably true that I hated losing even more than I loved winning.

But is winning a soccer match a matter of life and death? Not even close. The one true "life-and-death" battle was the one that secured our ultimate victory over our ultimate enemy. And we didn't even have to fight that battle.

In Peter's sermon in Jerusalem, after delivering the bad news that the people had murdered their Creator, Peter presented good news. The story hadn't ended with the cross: "**But God** raised Him up again, putting an end to the agony of death, since it was impossible for Him to be held in its power" (Acts 2:24).

You may have been wondering when the "But God . . ." was going to show up, and here it arrives in the most marvelous of ways. The God of surprise had accomplished the most unbelievable, most mysterious, and most eternally vital victory ever won. He had defeated death by dying.

Remember Peter's audience. The people of Israel had been conditioned to look for a powerful Rescuer, a mighty Messiah, a conquering King. But they would have never expected a crucified One. This was absolutely counterintuitive for the people of Jesus's day. They could not imagine a crucified Messiah. Yet that was the message of the gospel—and the mission of Christ: "fixing our eyes on Jesus, the author and perfecter of faith, who for the joy set before Him endured the cross, despising the shame, and has sat down at the right hand of the throne of God" (Hebrews 12:2).

The author of the letter to the Hebrews was writing to a Jewish audience and reminding them, as Peter had done at

Pentecost decades earlier, that the source of our joy and life is the One who knew the shame attached to His death and endured the horrors of it anyway.

Now, as they are overwhelmed by their crimes against the Christ, they are told the rest of the story. He is alive again and exalted at the side of the Father. For Jesus, His death was not the end of His life. It was the end of the reign of death over humanity. By taking the cross and conquering death, Jesus not only found His own joy but He also provided a platform for our joy. Death was conquered by resurrected life—bringing joy out of grief.

The point of all this? By Jesus's resurrection . . .

Death is conquered—to give us life now.
Death is conquered—to give us life forever.
Death is conquered—to restore the created order.
Death is conquered—to provide hope in our seasons
of grief.

The surprising truth is that the only way to defeat the power of death was for someone to die—and come back to life again. That is what Jesus did, which is the entire point of the only major theological section in Paul's first letter to Corinth—1 Corinthians 15. What Adam had produced in that first life-filled garden, Christ had destroyed by coming out of a garden tomb:

But now Christ has been raised from the dead, the first fruits of those who are asleep. For since by a man came death, by a man also came the resurrection of the dead. For as in Adam all die, so also in Christ all will be made alive. (1 Corinthians 15:20–22)

Paul went on to affirm: "The sting of death is sin, and the power of sin is the law; but thanks be to God, who gives us the victory through our Lord Jesus Christ" (1 Corinthians 15:56–57).

That is victory. Won for us when we were dead. Won for us by the Prince of life. Won for us at the highest cost and with the exertion of the greatest power.

We were without hope . . . but God.
We were doomed and deserving it . . . but God.
We were guilty and condemned . . . but God.

The Creator who had brought life into being had restored it in a most surprising way. The same Simon Peter would later write: "Blessed be the God and Father of our Lord Jesus Christ, who according to His great mercy has caused us to be born again to a living hope through the resurrection of Jesus Christ from the dead" (1 Peter 1:3).

Life's Second Chance

I began this chapter talking about officiating at my dad's funeral. But that wasn't the first time he had died—sort of. As a young man, my dad and his girlfriend were on a double date with another couple when their car skidded on wet, slick roads and crashed. Dad's girlfriend died at the scene, and he was declared dead. They put a toe tag on him and took him to the morgue in Roanoke, Virginia. My grandparents were called to identify the body, but after being presumed dead, dad revived. His parents were stunned to find him hurt and dazed, but very much alive.

I don't know if the misdiagnosis was due to the carnage of the wreck site or to the limited training and equipment available to first responders those many decades ago. But I know this—Dad went from what seemed to be the finality of death to a second chance at life. He would eventually meet my mom, and seven little Crowders later, there would be generations (including Marlene's and my five children and so far six grandkids) who would have never existed if death had won.

Don't get me wrong. I'm not saying Dad's experience in any way is the same as what Jesus secured by exiting the tomb. It is, however, a useful metaphor for the power of life. Life produces. Life builds. Life *lives*. And ultimately all of that life and living has a Source in the One who created life and then restored it with His own death. Edna R. Worrell put it this way:

The dawn of victory
Leaps thro' a night of gloom,
Piercing with living swords of flame,
The Savior's hallowed tomb.
Dawn of a glad new day,

Shining with holy light,
Glorifies the place from which the Lord
Is risen in His might.

Now, *that* is a victory worth celebrating.

Lord of life, I thank you for conquering death. I thank you for restoring the life that our rebellion had killed and for giving us the truest of all victories—the victory over death and the grave. I marvel at your wisdom and your perfect plan, and I pray that you would give me the wisdom, grace, and strength to live this gift of life in the name of the One who secured it and set me free.

Chapter Three

The Surprise
of God's Working

*But God has chosen the foolish things of
the world to shame the wise, and God
has chosen the weak things of the world
to shame the things which are strong.*

1 Corinthians 1:27

One of my favorite sports movies is *Miracle*, which recounts the story of the 1980 US Olympic men's hockey team. Coached by the now-legendary Herb Brooks, this team of college students went toe-to-toe with the greatest hockey team in the world—the Soviet Union—and came away winners in the Olympics semifinals. They would then go on to win the gold medal in what is still considered one of the greatest upsets in modern sports history.

A key moment in the film comes at the very beginning as players from across the country gather in Colorado Springs to try out for the squad. Quickly, however, Brooks settles on his team and shows the list to his assistant coach Craig Patrick. Patrick reads the list, and clearly surprised, says, "You're missing some of the best players." Brooks cagily responds,

"Not looking for the best players, Craig. I'm looking for the right ones."

That is a shocking approach to major sports. Usually, teams look for the *best* players, and nothing less will do.

Regarding football fans, the more passionate they are the more they are passionate about who their teams recruit to their sides. In American college football, national signing day every February is a day of intense drama as high school football players command the attention of the nation. Standing before the cameras, they smile wryly before pulling out a ball cap emblazoned with the logo of the school they plan to grace with their gridiron gifts.

For NFL fans, it is all about the NFL draft. After months of interviews, evaluation, and speculation, the teams announce the players upon whom they will shower millions of dollars. Depending upon the selection, each team's fan base either goes over the moon with celebration or goes ballistic in despair over the judgment of their team's collective brain trust.

For world football (soccer) fans, the processes are radically different, but the goals are essentially the same. How does a team strengthen its squad by bringing in the best players available and discharging some other players now deemed "surplus to requirements"? In the twice-yearly transfer windows, fans scour the gossip pages and look for any kind of hint that their team might be on the verge of a major signing.

This angst is not limited to the world of football. In the corporate world, people responsible for hiring also face a massive task. They must carefully examine the applicant's résumé, experience, education, skillset, and references, seeking a level of confidence that the individual will be a good fit for the opening being filled. Only time will tell if the effort invested will result in a good hire.

I have a sense of this because my dad once owned an employment agency, and my mom worked in the human resources department of a large company. Now our oldest son works in HR for a local newspaper. In my time as a pastor, I was also involved in hiring. When our young church was struggling to fill its first pastoral staff position, one of our leadership team cautioned, "If you think it's hard trying to hire a staff member, just wait until the first time you have to fire one." That was sobering with a capital S.

Nevertheless, on the hiring side of things, the task is clear-cut and simple. The goal is to find the most capable, most skilled, best trained candidate possible for each position—and that is extremely difficult.

A Different Approach

What I find so surprising is how counterintuitive our God is in this area as well. We look for the best and the brightest, the skilled and the savvy, the talented and the terrific. God is much more versatile. Consider Jesus's twelve disciples. Not a one of them would we consider for the role of executive leadership in a Fortune 500 corporation. They were "un"—unrefined, uneducated, untalented, unknown, and unprepared. Yet they would be God's instruments in taking the good news of Jesus to the world and establishing a global church.

The surprise of God's working is that He uses unlikely people to accomplish extraordinary things. We find this unexpected formula for ministry in 1 Corinthians 1:25–29, where Paul lays the groundwork for God's shocking plan:

> The foolishness of God is wiser than men, and the weakness of God is stronger than men. For consider your calling, brethren, that there were not many wise according to the flesh, not many mighty, not many noble; **but God** has chosen the foolish things of the world to shame the wise, and God has chosen the weak things of the world to shame the things which are strong, and the base things of the world and the despised God has chosen, the things that are not, so that He may nullify the things that are, so that no man may boast before God.

As we compare this selection grid to corporate hiring, player selection, or any sort of recruitment activity, it almost seems a little crazy. Why would you entrust the most important mission in the universe to those who appear to be the least capable of carrying it out? It seems reckless at best and foolish at worst. But read again verse 25: "The foolishness of God is wiser than men, and the weakness of God is stronger than men" (1 Corinthians 1:25).

Any consideration of God's working must be understood within the context of who is making these selections and empowering the work. What may appear foolish to us does not even begin to plumb God's great wisdom—a wisdom that is capable of using both great and small alike. As Herb Brooks said, "Not looking for the best players. I'm looking for the right ones."

God's Unsurprising Instruments

When Billy Graham died at the age of 99 following a lengthy illness in 2018, the tributes poured in from all over the world. The impact of his life globally was seemingly immeasurable, but it wasn't simply his impact that was lauded. Billy's unique blend of passion, humility, charisma, and giftedness made him a once-in-a-generation instrument in the hands of his God. And while many applauded the breadth of Billy Graham's influence, others speculated as to who could ever fill the void Graham's passing had left.

This is part of God's working that should be unsurprising to us, but it should still be acknowledged. We will see clearly that, as Christian recording artist Danniebelle Hall sang, "God uses ordinary people." But God is also well capable of using extraordinary ones. In 1 Corinthians this is very subtly acknowledged by Paul, who wrote: "For consider your calling, brethren, that there were not many wise according to the flesh, not many mighty, not many noble" (1:26).

The key here is that Paul says "not *many*." He does not say "not *any*." There is a place in kingdom work for the wise, the mighty, and the noble. The exceptional are not excluded. We see this in the case of the two men who buried the body of Jesus following the horrors of His crucifixion. Notice:

After these things Joseph of Arimathea, being a disciple of Jesus, but a secret one for fear of the Jews, asked Pilate that he might take away the body of Jesus; and Pilate granted permission. So he came and took away His body. Nicodemus, who had first come to Him by night, also came, bringing a mixture of myrrh and aloes, about a hundred pounds weight. So they took the body of Jesus and bound it in linen wrappings with the spices, as is the burial custom of the Jews. (John 19:38–40)

These two men would have been part of the power base of first-century Jerusalem. Joseph of Arimathea is described several ways—and all of them point to his high standing in the community.

Matthew 27:57 describes Joseph as being a rich man who had become a disciple of Jesus.

Mark 15:43 calls him, "a prominent member of the Council, who himself was waiting for the kingdom of God."

Luke 23:50–51 describes Joseph as a "good and righteous" man who, though a member of the council, had not "consented" to their plan to kill Jesus.

John refers to Joseph as a secret disciple of Jesus. Although his secrecy was rooted in his fear of his colleagues in the Jewish religious establishment, Joseph found the courage to defy the leaders of his nation and provide a proper burial for the slain Rabbi from Nazareth. And he was not alone.

John says that Joseph was assisted by Nicodemus, which should be shocking. John 3 says, "Now there was a man of the Pharisees, named Nicodemus, a ruler of the Jews; this man came to Jesus by night" (John 3:1–2). Jesus actually refers to Nicodemus as "the teacher of Israel" (John 3:10). *The* teacher of Israel. This is astounding. The leading teacher in Israel not only sought a private audience with Jesus but also publicly assisted in His burial.

Here you have two important, influential, and significant men of their day publicly identifying with Jesus at the worst possible moment. And not only do they identify with Jesus but they also serve Him in a most tangible and necessary way.

In history and in our generation, we are witnesses to the fact that God still uses men and women to accomplish His purposes in the world. For instance, a struggling abolitionist movement in England took flight when a follower of Christ who happened to be a member of Parliament embraced the cause. After years of struggle, slavery was ended in England. And there is that brilliant skeptic, Clive Staples Lewis, who at the time considered himself an atheist, yet he became one of the most influential Christian voices of the twentieth century.

Add to that the hospitals, schools, ministries, and other endeavors funded by highly successful business people whose wealth was leveraged for kingdom purposes, and there is no doubt that the wise, the mighty, and the noble are not excluded from participating in the work of God on the earth.

But while they are not *excluded*, they are the *exception*.

God's Shocking Vessels

> **But God** has chosen the foolish things of the world to shame the wise, and God has chosen the weak things of the world to shame the things which are strong, and the base things of the world and the despised God has chosen, the things that are not, so that He may nullify the things that are. (1 Corinthians 1:27–28)

And our ever-valuable "But God . . ." is now clearly seen in its context. This is absolutely intended to surprise us. To shock us. To make us scratch our heads. The high and mighty are not the norm. The *norm* is the norm. The average become instruments to accomplish the extraordinary.

For the most important task in human history, we would expect the most important people to be chosen. But God intentionally uses the unexpected and the unremarkable—and this highlights some very important ideas about spiritual service.

First, we cannot skip past the words "has chosen." God's determination to use the seemingly unusable has been done with extreme intentionality. God's usage of ordinary folks is not a fallback plan in the event someone more talented isn't available. Far from being a fallback plan, God's use of the average and the unexceptional *is* the plan.

Second, what the world finds useless, God uses in ways that confound conventional wisdom. Paul uses words like *shame* and *nullify*. Why? To remind us that the things that are accomplished are not for our own personal praise or acclaim. They are done by God's grace and wisdom, not by our personal skill or cleverness—evidenced by the apparently inadequate tools God chooses.

The result of all of this is that our confidence must be in Him, not in ourselves. To that end, Paul says that God does it this way "so that no man may boast before God" (1 Corinthians 1:29).

Perhaps the classic example of this idea would be Dwight L. Moody, the great evangelist whose preaching, by God's grace, shook nations on both sides of the Atlantic in the 1800s. Lacking formal education and famously criticized for his inarticulate grammar, Moody was used of God to see hundreds come to Christ. His influence has been recognized by the Chicago Avenue Church being renamed the Moody Church, and the Chicago Bible Institute becoming the Moody Bible Institute.

But there are countless other examples of God's powerful use of the ordinary. Everyday folks who serve in soup kitchens, travel abroad to build church buildings, engage in medical missions, invest their limited resources in shaping young lives with the gospel, and the list goes on and on. It is more than just an army of regular men and women. It is a global body.

The Picture of the Body

There is strength in numbers and there is power in unity. This is clearly seen in the US Olympic hockey team we considered in the opening of this chapter. When they faced off against the Soviet Union, they were outmanned and outgunned. The Soviet squad contained the most talented players in the world and had largely been together for a decade. The American squad was young, inexperienced, and in over their heads. But while the Soviet Union had great players, the USA team played great as a team.

Compare this to how the body of Christ is described later in 1 Corinthians 12:22–25, and again Paul utilizes "but God . . ." to make his point:

> On the contrary, it is much truer that the members of the body which seem to be weaker are necessary; and those members of the body which we deem less honorable, on these we bestow more abundant honor, and our less presentable members become much more presentable, whereas our more presentable members have no need of it. **But God** has so composed the body, giving more abundant honor to that member which lacked, so that there may be no division in the body, but that the members may have the same care for one another.

The twin realities of God's counterintuitive working is that all of us are dependent upon Him, and all of us are interdependent upon one another. This is how God works and how any of us can become useful in His working. Understanding that we have a role in the body of Christ and how that role fits into the body are terrific challenges that we must embrace.

Why? Because every child of God has a part to play in the work God is doing in His world. While some areas of service (and the giftedness that supports them) seem to be of higher profile or greater significance, God places "abundant honor" (1 Corinthians 12:24) on the roles that we might tend to ignore. While unnoticed by men, every act of service done in Jesus's name has value. Our Lord himself said:

> Then the righteous will answer Him, "Lord, when did we see You hungry, and feed You, or thirsty, and give You something to drink? And when did we see You a stranger, and invite You in, or naked, and clothe You? When did we see You sick, or in prison, and come to You?" The King will answer and say to them, "Truly I say to you, to the extent that you did it to one of these brothers of Mine, even the least of them, you did it to Me." (Matthew 25:37–40)

We serve as a body. We serve one another. We serve outsiders. We serve in His strength and provision. But as we do, most significantly, we serve Him. And the apostle Paul makes it clear that all of us are invited to participate in serving Him—together.

An Open Door

In this chapter, we have spent a fair amount of time in Paul's first letter to the Christ-followers at Corinth. In the final chapter of this letter, the apostle says:

> But I will remain in Ephesus until Pentecost; for a wide door for effective service has opened to me. (1 Corinthians 16:8–9)

That open door is not the private territory of brilliant apostles (as Paul surely was) or of the extraordinarily gifted (as Paul also was). Through the power of the Holy Spirit indwelling us and the spiritual giftedness (enablings) each of us have received, all of us have the opportunity to serve. All of us have an open door because we live in a terribly needy world. As Ira B. Wilson put it:

> Out in the highways and byways of life,
> Many are weary and sad;
> Carry the sunshine where darkness is rife,
> Making the sorrowing glad.
>
> Make me a blessing,
> Make me a blessing,
> Out of my life
> May Jesus shine;
> Make me a blessing, O savior, I pray,
> Make me a blessing to someone today.

That is the opportunity—the open door—available to each of us. What a privilege to serve in Jesus's name!

Lord, make me an instrument of your peace,
Where there is hatred, let me sow love;
Where there is injury, pardon;
Where there is doubt, faith;
Where there is despair, hope;
Where there is darkness, light;
Where there is sadness, joy.

The Prayer of St. Francis

Chapter Four

The Surprise
of Full Provision

*My flesh and my heart may fail, **but God** is the
strength of my heart and my portion forever.*

PSALM 73:26

I have heard so many stories like this that I always take them
with a grain of salt. Or a pinch of salt. Or maybe an entire
salt mine. But this happened to us, and while it may seem
outlandish, it is nevertheless true.

I was pastoring a small church and money was always
tight—sometimes beyond tight. Add into the mix a lovely
wife and four rambunctious kids. And they all expected to eat
on a regular basis. Plus, I was working on seminary classes
on the side.

Did I mention that money was tight?

At one point, it got *really* tight, even for us. It was several
days before payday, and we simply didn't have any food in
the house. Marlene and I were worried about how we were
going to put dinner on the table because we were out of options. As we stared at each other, the doorbell rang (this is
the part people usually take with a grain of salt). We went
to the door, and there was no one there. But there were two

bags of groceries. Enough to get us to payday. We had prayed about the situation, and we had not spoken of it to anyone else. Yet there those bags were!

It's interesting. No one gave us a check for thousands of dollars or paid off our maxed-out credit cards. There were no angelic choirs singing or loud peals of thunder. Just two extremely timely bags of groceries. It was enough for the need of that moment. And we did not have a second's doubt that God had answered our prayers. How He did it or who He used to accomplish it we will never know. But we *know* that God provided.

There have been many times in my years of walking with Christ when there were situations of need. Some of them quite severe. In the vast majority of those times there was no breathtaking moment of earth-shattering supply. Most of the time, the solutions were much more ordinary.

But those two bags of groceries!

That was the time that sticks with me. That was the time I'll never forget. That was the time that taught me an unforgettable lesson about God's provision. It is a lesson that a man in the Bible struggled with. A man named Asaph.

The Goodness of God

During the Israelites' trek through the wilderness, when Moses was on the mountain receiving the law, he requested of God, "I pray You, show me Your glory!" (Exodus 33:18). God's response was actually a little surprising.

And He said, "*I Myself will make all My goodness pass before you*, and will proclaim the name of the LORD before you; and I will be gracious to whom I will be gracious, and will show compassion on whom I will show compassion." (Exodus 33:19; emphasis added)

Moses asks to see God's glory, but God shows him His goodness. This is a big idea. God's goodness is one of the most important things about Him—for, as He told Moses, from that goodness flows God's compassion and grace. Little wonder then that this is the place where we begin when our hearts are troubled. When we are struggling. When we don't have answers that can match the magnitude of the challenges we face. We look to the goodness of God, and we trust that He will provide compassion and grace.

This was also the place where Asaph began in his song that gives a very different take on God's provision. He wrote in Psalm 73: "Surely God is good to Israel, to those who are pure in heart!" (Psalm 73:1).

Asaph, by the way, was no ordinary singer or psalmist. He was one of the key worship leaders for the nation of Israel (1 Chronicles 16:5). With that in mind, it would seem fairly normal to hear him praising God's goodness. But what we need to understand is this: While this is the first declaration of his song, it is actually the conclusion Asaph has reached after a difficult season of life. He had been questioning the very goodness of the God he was leading people to worship, but now he has learned better.

Asaph gives us his conclusion first—God is good. But it took him a while to get there. In the rest of Psalm 73 Asaph tells us his journey back to God's goodness.

The Comparison Game

Envy. Jealousy. Two of the ugliest words in the English language and two of the most destructive of human emotions. In *The Call*, Os Guinness writes:

> Traditionally envy was regarded as the second worst and second most prevalent of the seven deadly sins. Like pride, it is a sin of the spirit, not the flesh, and thus a "cold" and highly "respectable" sin, in contrast to the "warm" and openly "disreputable" sins of the flesh, such as gluttony. Its uniqueness lies in the fact that it is the one vice that its perpetrators never enjoy and rarely confess.

He then added:

> Like pride, envy by its very nature is comparative and competitive. Or more precisely, pride is competitive and envy is the result of pride wounded in competition. As C. S. Lewis wrote in *Mere Christianity*, "Pride is essentially competitive. . . . Pride gets no pleasure out of having something, only out of having more of it than the next man. We say people are proud of

being rich, or clever, or good-looking, but they are not. They are proud of being richer, or cleverer, or better-looking than others."

As such, envy is not simply about what *we* lack. It is also about what *they* have. What *they* have in comparison to what *we* lack. And how we feel about that. So, when Asaph begins to tell us his story, he starts with how he felt about what others had and what he felt he was being deprived of. It's not a pretty sight.

But as for me, my feet came close to stumbling, My steps had almost slipped. For I was envious of the arrogant as I saw the prosperity of the wicked. (Psalm 73:2–3)

We often applaud honesty, but frankly, this level of candor can be unsettling. In our generation, we expect our spiritual leaders to be brimming with confidence in God and absolute certainty of His character. I would suspect that the people of Asaph's day expected something similar from him. But that was not his heart.

Read Psalm 73:4–11, and you will find that Asaph observes those he calls "wicked" and the prosperity they are enjoying. He sees them blessed with more than a heart can desire, and he struggles under the inequity of it all. On top of that, the prosperous wicked mock God the entire time they are enjoying the abundance Asaph doesn't have. He is jealous. He is envious of the wicked as he observes their prosperity (v. 3).

Far from trusting in the goodness of God, Asaph described his heart as having been riddled with doubt—and the worship leader of Israel was angry about his own inability to trust God.

The Issue of Motive

During Jesus's years of public ministry, He turned the thinking of His generation upside down in a variety of ways. He drove His hearers from the letter of the law to the spirit of the law. He included the marginalized and the outcasts. He not only preached about loving your enemies but He also modeled it perfectly. The King of an upside-down kingdom was turning the tables on His times—both literally and figuratively.

Yet, one of the most significant surprises of Jesus's surprising ministry was that He was constantly driving people to examine their motives. The law told them what they were to do. Jesus was more concerned about *why* they did or did not do it. He asked questions like:

Why do you call Me, "Lord, Lord," and do not do what I say? (Luke 6:46)

Why do you call Me good? No one is good except God alone. (Mark 10:18)

The *why* questions are always the most difficult ones, in part because we struggle to know our own hearts. The Old Testament prophet Jeremiah states the problem clearly: "The heart is more deceitful than all else and is desperately sick; who can understand it?" (Jeremiah 17:9).

That includes us. In much of life—even in our best moments—it is likely that our motives are mixed, to some degree. Asaph's motives clearly were confused. He is envious of the wicked because of what they *have*, while not really giving enough attention to what they *were*. All Asaph is certain about is that they got theirs, but he hadn't gotten his! He says:

> Behold, these are the wicked; and always at ease, they have increased in wealth. Surely in vain I have kept my heart pure and washed my hands in innocence; for I have been stricken all day long and chastened every morning. (Psalm 73:12–14)

Is that it? Do we do right in order to do well? Do we serve God so He will reward us with an overflow of abundance? If we are honest, in the very least, we should probably say, "Sometimes." Whether it is tabulated as rewards in heaven or prosperity on earth, there seems to be an implicit "what's in it for me?" behind what we say and do in Jesus's name—and that's the problem.

The God we see in the Scriptures is worthy of our best service because He is good. Because He loves and forgives. Because His love endures forever. Because He is God. That should be enough—but if we were as candid as Asaph, we'd probably have to admit that we often have mixed motives as well.

What challenged Asaph to examine his motives is what should likewise challenge us—the most real reality in the universe. The Reality we encounter in worship. The reality of the eternal. It was when Asaph entered the sanctuary that his perspective changed. Asaph sings: "When I pondered to understand this, it was troublesome in my sight until I came into the sanctuary of God; then I perceived their end (Psalm 73:16–17).

Who knows how long Asaph had battled with his envy and doubts? As the worship leader, who knows how many times he had entered the sanctuary to do a job he wasn't sure he believed in anymore? But *this* time Asaph has an encounter with God that alters his perspective and moves him forward, restoring his waning confidence in God.

What did Asaph learn in the sanctuary of the eternal God? He learned that *now* is not all there is—and the end of the "wicked" (described in vv. 18–20) is not something to be desired. It is only when Asaph takes the long view that he understands that his jealousy has been misapplied. Instead of envying the prosperous wicked, he should be pitying them.

So Asaph moves. From jealousy to trust. From self-centeredness to self-examination. From thinking about provision to focusing on the Provider.

The God Who Provides

One of the most shocking events in the Old Testament—especially for any parent who loves his or her children—is the story of Abraham and Isaac in Genesis 22. There we read that God was testing Abraham to see how strongly he trusted in God. The test? Offer Isaac as a sacrifice to God for no other reason than that God said so. For many of us, that is the moment we would be most severely tempted to jump ship. Not Abraham.

Abraham takes his son Isaac to the mountain God showed him. The servants are left behind after Abraham tells them that he and the boy are going up to worship and will return. Remember that Isaac is not only Abraham's son (as if that weren't enough), but he is also the seed of God's promise to make a great nation of Abraham's offspring. All of God's promises to Abraham of a posterity and a people are bound up in that one young life. Clearly, Isaac is confused, because they have everything they need for worship except the most important part—the lamb to be sacrificed. When he asks his father about it, Abraham responds: "God will provide for Himself the lamb for the burnt offering, my son" (Genesis 22:8).

As you probably already know, God does provide a lamb. Abraham and Isaac worship. And the place of that sacrifice receives a new name. "Abraham called the name of that place The LORD Will Provide, as it is said to this day, 'In the mount of the LORD it will be provided'" (Genesis 22:14).

He named the place "Jehovah Jireh," which is Hebrew for "the Lord who provides." That's what Abraham believed as he and Isaac scaled the mountain, and that was what he believed when they made their way back down together later. It wasn't simply about the provision, it was about the Provider. *Jehovah Jireh.* The Lord who provides.

In Psalm 73, Asaph needed to get to that point as well. Until he saw the goodness, the provision, and the care of his God, he would never be truly convinced that "God is good" (see again v. 1). This was the lesson—and this, if you have been wondering, is where we discover the "But God . . ." surprise.

> Whom have I in heaven but You?
> And besides You, I desire nothing on earth.
> My flesh and my heart may fail,
> **But God** is the strength of my heart and my portion forever. . . .
> But as for me, the nearness of God is my good;
> I have made the Lord GOD my refuge,
> That I may tell of all Your works. (Psalm 73:25–26, 28)

This is the vast, unimaginable surprise of provision. God provides, but God himself is our ultimate provision! Asaph describes this in two ways, both of which are expressed in other psalms as well:

The strength of my heart. "I love You, O LORD, my strength." (Psalm 18:1)

My portion forever. "I cried out to You, O LORD; I said, 'You are my refuge, my portion in the land of the living.'" (Psalm 142:5)

The point Asaph makes is overwhelming in its importance. What we have *in* God is far more significant than what we get *from* God. This is perhaps why so many of us struggle with the idea of contentment. Especially in western cultures, contentment is secured by accumulation of things—but there is never enough. Accumulation of things is like drinking salt water; it only leaves us thirsty for more. And more. And more.

Contentment for the child of God is not based on what we have but rather on whose we are and who He is. It is this fundamental reality that fuels how our hearts are to process life in an often unfair world. It is not simply about what He does or what He provides, it is about who He is. Hebrews 13:5 says to be "content with what you have; for He Himself has said, 'I WILL NEVER DESERT YOU, NOR WILL I EVER FORSAKE YOU.'"

While the Scriptures have much to say about being content, the reason for our contentment is clear—in God we have all we need and more, even if it doesn't seem that way at the moment. If we stop and think about it, this only makes sense. He is the Creator of the universe, and the owner and possessor of all that is. He is life and breath and help and hope. He is everything.

Consider the apostle Paul as he writes the book of Philippians. He is under house arrest in Rome, and he had earlier endured beatings, imprisonment, stonings, and much, much more. Yet, under conditions that are far from ideal, he is able to write:

> Not that I speak from want, for I have learned to be content in whatever circumstances I am. I know how to get along with humble means, and I also know how

to live in prosperity; in any and every circumstance I
have learned the secret of being filled and going hun-
gry, both of having abundance and suffering need. I
can do all things through Him who strengthens me.
(Philippians 4:11–13)

This is critical. We often hear verses 11 and 13 quoted,
but usually they are quoted separately—and that misses
the point completely. The reason Paul is able to be content
(v. 11) in the midst of adverse and difficult circumstances is
his connection with Christ—the One who not only provides
his strength (v. 13) but He also *is* his strength. The two ideas
cannot be separated.

As Asaph and Paul had both learned through the hard
lessons of life, this is the great lesson of life—God is enough.
He himself is all of the provision we need, both now and
forever. And that is why Asaph could begin his song of frustration and discontent with a statement of God's goodness:
"Surely God is good to Israel, to those who are pure in heart!"
(Psalm 73:1).

God's goodness is sure because it is about who He is. It
is not simply what He does. As our strength and portion, we
find in Him all we truly need.

The Heart of a Child

The story is told of a small boy who came home from church
on a Sunday. When his father asked him what he had learned

in Sunday school, the boy responded, "We learned about the twenty-third Psalm." This prompted his dad to probe a bit further. "What did you learn about it?"

The boy's answer was priceless. He said, "The Lord is my shepherd. He's all I want."

That is the lesson. He's all I want. Moses learned it on a mountain. Abraham learned it on the way to a sacrifice. Paul learned it while imprisoned. Asaph learned it in the sanctuary. I learned it from two bags of groceries.

Hymnwriter George W. Robinson must have learned it as well, for he wrote:

Loved with everlasting love,
Led by grace that love to know;
Gracious Spirit from above,
Thou hast taught me it is so!
Oh, this full and perfect peace!
Oh, this transport all divine!
In a love which cannot cease,
I am His, and He is mine;
In a love which cannot cease,
I am His, and He is mine.

I am His and He is mine. How amazing is that!

Loving Lord, forgive me for my all-too-frequent tendency to look at what others have rather than all that I have in you. Teach me the lessons of contentment that finds my deepest satisfaction in who you are, not what I have. Thank you for loving me with everlasting love—show me the "enoughness" of that love.

Chapter Five

The Surprise
of Long Preparation

As for you, you meant evil against me, **but God**
meant it for good in order to bring about this
present result, to preserve many people alive.

GENESIS 50:20

One of the most fascinating people of the twentieth century was Helen Keller. Immortalized in the film *The Miracle Worker*, Helen's story is one of inspiration and endurance—seemingly beyond human capacity.

As a baby, Helen suffered a fever that made her both blind and deaf, giving her little opportunity for a "normal" life. Then a teacher named Anne Sullivan was brought into the picture to help Helen cope with her personal isolation, and the two began a long journey together. It was a journey marked by frustration, anger, helplessness, hopelessness, and almost limitless challenges. But this long journey had a destination.

Over the years of Sullivan's tutelage, Helen learned to communicate and slowly found herself reconnected with the human race from which she had been so distanced. Later, Helen Keller became the first deaf and blind person to graduate with a bachelor of arts degree. She became a political activist, an author, and a lecturer. Helen's long journey to communication had paid extraordinary benefits—but there was not a moment of that journey that was anything less than a pure struggle, prompting Helen Keller to write:

> Character cannot be developed in ease and quiet. Only through experience of trial and suffering can the soul be strengthened, ambition inspired, and success achieved.

Two things strike me as I consider Helen's words. First, she was not speaking out of a vacuum. Nothing about her words is in the slightest bit theoretical. Her entire life experience had been fueled by the rage she felt at her personal isolation. The long years of Helen's learning and Anne's mentoring were marked by trial and error—seasons of failure punctuated by an occasional brief moment of a successful breakthrough. The deeply personal experience of Helen's long journey gave her an authoritative platform from which to speak about "trial and suffering."

The second thought, however, gets more to the point of what we want to consider here. The unspoken truth behind Helen's profoundly true words is that often the process of growth takes time. It is slow and deliberate. It involves perseverance and endurance. And in order for endurance to reach some kind of meaningful aim, it requires a person to hold out hope that somehow, some way things will get better.

It requires waiting.

In the Waiting

In Psalm 13, Israel's David is crying out a lament. He is being pursued by enemies on all fronts, and though the psalm doesn't tell us the specifics of the danger, it is painfully clear that the peril is real. Perhaps this is David as a young man being hated and chased by King Saul because he sees David as a threat to his throne. Or quite possibly this is David being hounded by his own son, Absalom, because he has come to see his father as unfit for the throne. The specifics aren't given.

What we are given, however, is the root of David's pain. The pressure point from which he can find no relief. David sings:

> How long, O LORD? Will You forget me forever?
> How long will You hide Your face from me?
> How long shall I take counsel in my soul,
> Having sorrow in my heart all the day?
> How long will my enemy be exalted over me?
> (Psalm 13:1–2)

Notice that in these two verses David is complaining to God. Not only is he lamenting the enemies that pursue him and seek his life but he is also frustrated by God's apparent lack of interest in his situation. Four times in these two verses, David asks his God, "How long?" The natural despair of being hated and hounded is amplified by the fact that the experience feels as if it will never end. When there is a light at the end of the tunnel, hope is an option. When there appears to be no end in sight, it makes it all the more difficult to endure.

How long, O Lord?

In my years of pastoral ministry, I stood with many a grieving family who were forced to say goodbye to a loved one. In those experiences, I noticed something of a pattern to the difficulty of letting go.

In the days following the death, the blur of activity often issued into a numbness that held tears just below the surface. But as the days continued, there was a sense that nothing could ever be worse than this. No pain could ever be worse than this pain. No heartache greater than this heartache.

During the memorial service and the committal at the gravesite, a sense of finality would sometimes cause both confusion and a strange sense of guilty relief, especially when they had walked with their loved one through a long season of suffering. Meanwhile, the still-fresh, still-raw emotions were barely held at bay by the support of loved ones and caring friends. As the family slowly walked away from the place of death, they would begin to process the steps needed to at least attempt to resume life. To get back to normal.

But normal is no longer available. There is only a new normal, requiring moment by moment adjustments and acceptance that normal is gone forever because a significant part of normal is gone and will never return in this life.

How long?

For the rest of your life. The old normal can never be reclaimed. A new, different, foreign, and unwanted normal marks the long, long days and even longer nights ahead.

When life is long and we can't find the *why* to endure, let alone the *how*, what do we do? Where do we turn? How do we cope? As David demonstrated when he wrestled with this in his own interminable struggle, where does God fit into all of this?

Looking for God's Hand

Philip Yancey hit a massive, throbbing nerve in the lives of countless men and women when he released the book *Where Is God When It Hurts?* During enduring seasons of struggle, we want to know that God, though unseen, is nevertheless involved in the events that are the cause of our pain—events that are clearly beyond our control.

In those moments when we can't find God in the struggle, we are, spiritually, in a very vulnerable place. Simone Weil wrote, "Affliction makes God appear to be absent for a time, more absent than a dead man, more absent than light in the utter darkness of a cell. A kind of horror submerges the whole soul."

To help us find our way along this troubling path, I would direct you to the first book of the Bible, and to Joseph, my all-time favorite Bible character (aside from the Lord himself). In Genesis 37, we encounter the troubled, fractious family of the patriarch, Jacob (Israel). Jacob, himself a veteran of the interpersonal wars known as sibling rivalry, creates another such rivalry among his own sons by showing unabashed favoritism for Joseph, the first son of his much-favored wife, Rachel (a story for another time).

As a result, the brothers hate Joseph (v. 4) with a hatred that only unrequited love can generate. Unable to gain their father's love, these men decide to destroy what they perceive to be the obstacle to that love—their own half-brother, Joseph. They conspire to sell the seventeen-year-old into slavery in Egypt (vv. 27ff), and they truly believe that they are rid of this problem child and the massive problem he represents.

Sadly, nothing changes in Jacob's household. Jacob simply promotes Joseph's younger brother, Benjamin, to most-favored status. The older brothers still do not know their father's love. But while it seems that nothing is happening in Canaan, God is very much at work in Egypt. A process has begun—a process of long preparation that will mold and shape Joseph's character through the heartache, loneliness, betrayal, and treachery he will experience.

Perhaps the key to that preparation is found in Genesis 39. Joseph rises to a place of prominence in the house of his master, Potiphar, and then is imprisoned on false charges. He has been in Egypt about ten years, experiencing the hardships of slavery and rising above it. Even when he is falsely imprisoned, Joseph shows heart and character that is shocking for someone who has been treated as he has.

The key? In Genesis 39, we read four statements of God's presence with Joseph (vv. 2, 3, 21, 23) in hard times and good times, when rising and when falling, when suffering and when celebrating.

"The LORD was with Joseph," those passages tell us.

The one constant through it all was the presence of God. While living in hostile and foreign territory, Joseph remained in God's presence and grew to develop into the man he would have never become in Jacob's tents, where he was favored and pampered by his father. He became a leader, a ruler, a master of logistics, and the second most powerful man in Egypt, the most powerful nation on earth at that time.

The transformation of this young man's life was captured well by the great London pastor of the mid nineteenth century F. B. Meyer, who wrote:

> As a boy, Joseph's character tended to softness. He was a little spoilt by his father. He was too proud of his dreams and his foreshadowed greatness. None of these were great faults, but lacked the strength, grip, and power to rule. But, what a difference his imprisonment made in him! From that moment, he carries himself with modesty, wisdom, courage, and manly resolution that never fails him. He has learned to hold his peace and wait—surely the iron has entered his soul!

With all that Joseph went through, he could have been the poster child for A. W. Tozer's famous quote, "It is doubtful whether God can bless a man greatly until He has hurt him deeply."

But in the case of Joseph, it was not a sudden smashing that God allowed. Rather, it was a slow grinding that took place over the space of thirteen years. Thirteen years of loneliness and labor, accusation and abandonment, imprisonment and isolation. Thirteen years. I would encourage you to pause and ask yourself where you were and what you were doing thirteen years ago. Reflect on all of the life you have lived in this past baker's dozen of years. Consider just how long thirteen years is.

The "how long" of David had endured for years as well, but in Joseph's case, living in the presence of his God helped him to endure—and it was worth the wait. Named the vice-chancellor of Egypt and given a wife who gave him two sons, Joseph was no longer alone. And still fully aware of God's never-failing engagement with him all along the way, Joseph acknowledges God's hand of *blessing* in his life with the names he gave his sons:

> Joseph named the firstborn Manasseh, "For," he said, "God has made me forget all my trouble and all my father's household." He named the second Ephraim, "For," he said, "God has made me fruitful in the land of my affliction." (Genesis 41:51–52)

Manasseh and Ephraim. Forgetful and Fruitful. Or as J. Vernon McGee (1904–1988), one of my favorite Bible teachers for many years, put it, Amnesia and Ambrosia. The long years of preparation have now established Joseph in a pivotal place. He has lived out Isaiah's words centuries before the prophet uttered them:

Yet those who wait for the LORD will gain new strength; they will mount up with wings like eagles, they will run and not get tired, they will walk and not become weary. (Isaiah 40:31)

Joseph can clearly see God's hand in his experiences—even the hard ones. The pain-filled ones. Yet all of this was allowed—not only to build Joseph into the man he became but also to make him a part of a plan Joseph could have never imagined. And neither could his brothers.

Looking for God's Plan

The old TV series *The A-Team* followed a disgraced group of soldiers who, like Joseph, had been falsely accused. Having gone underground to escape incarceration, these four soldiers found themselves constantly thrust into situations where they helped folks who were in trouble, usually because they were oppressed by powerful, corrupt men.

The show was half action, half comedy, and all tongue-in-cheek as over-the-top chaos was the dominant theme of every episode. Then, in the final moments of each show, all of the pieces would fall into place. The good guys (that would be the A-Team, of course) would win, the bad guys would go to jail, and justice would prevail. And somewhere along the way, in the midst of all of that chaos, Col. Hannibal Smith, the A-Team's leader, would crow, "I love it when a plan comes together."

What works on TV doesn't always seem to work in life. In the difficult times of life, it can be hard to imagine that there even is a plan, let alone try to imagine that it is somehow coming together. Long seasons of struggle tend to blunt our faith and test our confidence in God. But Joseph's story reminds us that even in the darkest experiences imaginable there is a plan.

This is the "But God . . ." moment. The awakening to a purpose behind all the other purposes. A reason that takes the unreasonable circumstances of life and gives them extraordinary worth.

Joseph's rise to power in Egypt was connected to his prophetic interpretation of Pharaoh's dreams—dreams of a coming worldwide famine. It is Joseph who maps out a plan for a different kind of long preparation. The skills he learned in his years managing Potiphar's household were now being leveraged on a global scale. As the seven-year famine begins, there is hope for the starving because there is food in Egypt.

When the world comes to Egypt looking for food (Genesis 41:57), Joseph is ready to distribute the provisions the Egyptians have accumulated. And when the world comes looking for food, that includes the people of Canaan—and Joseph's own family. To be more specific, the brothers who had sold him into slavery. Through a series of encounters, Joseph conceals his identity from his brothers and tests them. He knows that the Lord has been at work in his heart in Egypt. Perhaps he wonders if his God has also been at work in his family back home.

It is a fascinating reunion story and well worth reading (Genesis 42–45), but the key moment for us comes when Joseph finally reveals his identity. Now he is in a position of power. Now he is the one with all the might at his disposal. At this revelation, the brothers are understandably "dismayed" (Genesis 45:3). They must have wondered, "What kind of revenge will Joseph extract for all that we did to him?"

But just as Joseph has lived in God's presence and experienced God's hand, he has also learned to trust God's plan. On the macro level, God's plan was to save the world from famine and provide for starving people (Genesis 45:7). But on the micro scale, in an intensely personal way, God's plan was to restore this tragically dysfunctional family. To heal hearts that had known, by this time, some twenty-two years of unremitting guilt for having sold Joseph into slavery. To heal the broken relationships that seemed beyond hope and help.

Seeing their despair, Joseph does not hesitate. The God of surprise has been in control, and that is the indisputable fact that Joseph clings to. God's plan of restoration has come together, and though the brothers may be dumbfounded by all that has transpired, Joseph's confidence is absolute—so much so that he chooses forgiveness over payback. He chooses restoration over revenge.

To underline this deep-seated conviction, Joseph twice affirms that his long years of preparation in Egypt had purpose. He says to his brothers:

Now, therefore, it was not you who sent me here, **but God**; and He has made me a father to Pharaoh and

lord of all his household and ruler over all the land
of Egypt. (Genesis 45:8)

And later, after the death of their father Jacob, Joseph
reaffirms his confidence in God's surprising purposes:

As for you, you meant evil against me, **but God** meant
it for good in order to bring about this present result,
to preserve many people alive. (Genesis 50:20)

"But God . . ." What powerful words to apply to the life
experiences that we don't understand!

Philosopher Søren Kierkegaard sagely said, "Life can only
be understood backwards; but it must be lived forwards." Joseph
looks back with clear understanding. His brothers' evil intent
could not thwart God's perfect purposes, so Joseph's prepared
heart moves to a forgiveness that resolves the problem of their
guilt. In *The Bible Knowledge Commentary*, commentator
A. P. Ross wrote of Joseph's forgiving words:

The certainty that God's will, not man's, is the controlling
reality in every event shined through as the basis for
reconciliation. No doubt Joseph had consoled himself
many times with this principle of faith. He who is
spiritual can perceive the hand of God in every event,
and therefore is able to forgive those who wrong him.

Bible teacher J. A. Sailhammer, in *The Expositor's Bible
Commentary*, affirmed:

Those words pull back the narrative veil and allow the reader to see what has been going on behind the scenes all along. It was not the brothers who sent Joseph to Egypt; it was God—and God had a purpose for it all. We have seen numerous clues within the narrative that this has been the case; but now the central character, the one ultimately responsible for initiating the plots and subplots of the preceding narratives, reveals the divine plan behind it all. Joseph, who could discern the divine plan in the dreams of Pharaoh, also knows the divine plan in the affairs of his brothers. God's plan is accomplishing a "great deliverance." (Genesis 45: 7)

"But God . . ."

The long years of preparation had produced a heart that could lead, but also a heart that could forgive. That is how powerful God's purposes are, for it is not Joseph or the brothers who are in view here—the focus is on the sovereign Lord and His heart lived out by His servants who trust Him. What seemed hopeless could have destroyed Joseph, "but God" was present. God was at work, and in the end it is clear that Joseph felt that it was worth it.

The God of surprise had produced more than they could have ever dreamed.

A Journey of Trust

This patient trust over the long haul is not the easiest perspective to add to our worldview. But being able to rest in God's purposes and being able to trust God's timing can allow the "how long" seasons of life to be strengthened and enriched by the presence of the God of surprise.

It is the confident trust that somehow allowed concentration camp survivor Corrie Ten Boom to forgive her Nazi tormentors.

It is the hopeful faith that allowed Horatio G. Spafford to write "It Is Well with My Soul" following the tragic deaths of his four daughters.

It is the spiritual discipline that enables us to actively look for the "but God . . ." in our moments of struggle and strife.

At its core, we are encouraged to look for the God of surprise in all the circumstances of life—and trust that His perfect plan will come together. As the hymnwriter put it,

Tis so sweet to trust in Jesus,
Just to take Him at His Word,
Just to rest upon His promise,
Just to know, "Thus saith the Lord."
Jesus, Jesus how I trust Him,
How I've proved Him o'er and o'er.
Jesus, Jesus, precious Jesus!
Oh, for grace to trust Him more.

Purposeful Father, I confess that much of the time I just don't get it. I'm blind to your purposes and ignorant of your plans. In those moments, Lord, remind me that the one thing I can be absolutely certain about is your love. Help me to receive the moments of life as expressions of your purposes, to be lived out in your presence. And when I am confused and discouraged, give me grace to trust you more. And more. And more.

Chapter Six

The Surprise
of God's Comfort

But God, who comforts the depressed,
comforted us by the coming of Titus.

2 CORINTHIANS 7:6

For several years, it was my privilege to pastor a small church in southern California. The church was filled with wonderful people who loved Christ and simply wanted a place to serve Him. Through no fault of their own, it was also a group that had experienced a series of heartbreaking setbacks. By the time the church was seven years old, average attendance had grown to almost 600, and in addition to other major ministry efforts, the church had built a Christian school to serve their own children and the kids within the community. It seemed that everything they attempted had been already touched with God's favor.

Then the church's two pastors had a falling out. The falling out became increasingly acrimonious, and ultimately a split resulted. Suddenly, the vibrant, dynamic congregation had dropped to about 150 in attendance and had lost its facilities and the school it had birthed. The people were meeting in a rented commercial building, and survival was the priority—though admittedly, some in the church family struggled to see why congregational survival even mattered at that point.

The day my family and I arrived at Los Angeles International Airport, Patty (the church secretary and all-around whiz of the place) picked us up at the airport, deposited Marlene and the kids at the lovely house the church had secured for us, and took me to the office to get started. When we arrived, however, the door had been tagged by the city building commission. Apparently, the church had been meeting for the previous months in a building that was not zoned for churches and apparently never would be.

That sucker punch felt like a death blow to a group of Christ-followers who had already endured so much and was hanging on with their last reserves of determination. Already strapped financially by the losses the church had suffered, the people had to weigh the additional cost of a legal battle with the city against two equally ominous options—either close up shop and find other churches to attend or try to locate a new meeting place in the extremely expensive Greater Los Angeles real estate market.

I struggle to adequately express the state of despair my new friends and I felt. It was beyond hopeless. As the process unfolded, the following months were marked by a sense of dread that the inevitable was just waiting around the corner. But we continued on.

The feelings of most of the folks there were captured at Christmastime when our choir—small in numbers but substantial in willingness—presented a little Christmas musical. It went surprisingly well, but at its conclusion I saw the wife of one of our leaders off to the side of the auditorium alone—softly crying, I asked her, "Fran, are you okay?" She responded, "I had come to the conclusion that God didn't have any good things left for us. But tonight I began to wonder if maybe I was wrong about that."

There it is. A hope that is afraid to hope. A hope that struggles to see its way forward. As actor Henry Cavill said, "No matter what era we're in, we need hope." Knowing where to find that hope, knowing where to locate true comfort—that is the key.

Life's Debilitating Realities

The same empty, fearful expressions I had seen on the faces of my friends in Southern California were also clearly visible years later and half a world away during my first teaching trip to Russia.

The trip began with two weeks in Moscow, and my task was to teach a group of pastors. While most of these spiritual servants had already begun serving congregations, the restrictions of communism had prevented them from having any meaningful training for ministry. My repeated trips to Russia to offer instruction and preparation for these men and women was one of the richest experiences I have ever been allowed to have.

After that first teaching assignment was completed, I joined Bob Provost (then head of Slavic Gospel Association) on a trip into the Caucasus Mountains region of southern Russia, where civil war was raging between Russia and Chechnya. Our mission was to take food, clothing, and medicine to refugees who had been displaced by the conflict.

To this day, our first stop still haunts me. We came to a small house only sixty miles from where the battle was being fought, and there we found a group of twenty-seven women and children. They had fled their homes empty-handed. They had no idea where their husbands and fathers were, or even if they were still alive. The people we encountered that day were utterly and thoroughly broken. Hopeless. Without comfort.

The provisions we took them were not going to solve their problems. Those bags of food and clothing would not answer all of their questions. But it was a place to start. It was a faint ray of light cutting through the dull gray bleakness of their current circumstances.

Those Chechen women and children were Muslims. But as Bob shared the message of Jesus with them over a hastily brewed cup of tea, you could see the despair in their expressions shift to surprise as they realized that the aid had come to them from Christians—people they were supposed to view with deep skepticism.

What I saw in that ramshackle, jam-packed house near Chechnya that day I have seen all over the world. People crushed under the burdens of a world that seems irrevocably broken. The haunting looks and bent bodies. The eyes staring vacantly and the hearts drained of emotion. People without any reason to expect anything except more loss. People who had learned, with Job: "For man is born for trouble, as sparks fly upward" (Job 5:7). And "Man who is born of woman is of few days and full of trouble" (Job 14:1 NKJV).

Admittedly, few of us will experience loss and struggle on the same scale that Job did, but that doesn't minimize the weight of the personal struggles we each face. In person after person, story after story, family after family, the details of the individual experiences may change but the reality is the same. A world created for light and life, scarred by the fall and its devastating effects, is now more characterized by darkness and despair. For people living under the crushing weight of that darkness, it is easy to wonder why, if there actually is a God, He doesn't help. Why He doesn't comfort. Why He doesn't seem to care.

Though followers of Christ may sometimes wrestle with these same questions, the Bible offers us a place to go for answers. In the Scriptures, we see God intervening in the human experience. But even more, we see comfort—not as a task on a heavenly to-do list but as an essential element of God's character.

God's Comforting Nature

Admittedly, it would be impossible to absolutely define the God of the universe within the limitations of human language. But if you were asked to define God with one word, what word would you choose?

Some would pick "holy" to speak of the set-apartness of God, which makes Him distinct and separate from His creation and His creatures.

Some would select "sovereign" to remind us that God rules and reigns absolutely over the heavens and the earth.

Some would choose "powerful" to explore His immeasurable ability that we see evidenced in the things He has made.

Some would suggest "love," in order to keep before us the wonder that everything God does in us and for us are expressions of the perfect, faithful, unbreakable love He has for us.

Clearly, none of those ideas is incorrect—but all are ultimately inadequate because God can't be fully captured in a single word. Still, that didn't keep Paul from offering his answer to the question.

Of all the churches Paul served, wrote to, or planted, arguably none was more troubled or troublesome than the church at Corinth. We have two of his letters to Corinth in the Scriptures. In the second one, Paul opens with his one-word description of God: comfort.

> Blessed be the God and Father of our Lord Jesus Christ, the Father of mercies and God of all *comfort*, who *comforts* us in all our affliction so that we will be able to *comfort* those who are in any affliction with the *comfort* with which we ourselves are *comforted* by God. (2 Corinthians 1:3–4; emphasis added)

Given the combative nature of Paul's relationship with the Corinthian congregation, it is remarkable that he seeks to speak into that conflict with words of comfort about the God of comfort. To be fair, for all of their problems, the Corinthians were apparently a small, embattled group living in deeply hostile territory. Life as a Christ–follower in Corinth would have been extremely challenging, so for all of their differences and disagreements, Paul understood that they needed to discover what he was continually learning—God gives His comfort to us, allowing us to then be His vessels of comfort to others.

As we will see, Paul knew from his own experiences that God is able to personally give comfort. But he also knew that God's comfort was a theme that was integral to the testimony of the Scriptures. Notice (emphasis added):

Even though I walk through the valley of the shadow of death, I fear no evil, for You are with me; Your rod and Your staff, they *comfort* me. (Psalm 23:4)

May Your lovingkindness *comfort* me. (Psalm 119:76)

Going on in the fear of the Lord and in the *comfort* of the Holy Spirit, it continued to increase. (Acts 9:31)

These are not just proof-texts, nor are they catchy snippets from random Scriptures. They are part of one of the great underlying themes of the Bible—the very theme Paul was tapping into in order to offer encouragement to the church at Corinth. God is not merely a comforting God—He is the God of all comfort. He is the endless, extraordinary wellspring from which we find mercy and "grace to help us in time of need" (Hebrews 4:16).

With all of that in view, we must grasp the fact that Paul's presentation of God's comfort to the Corinthians is surprising. In a letter in which he will respond to attacks on his character, questions about his apostolic role, and doubts about his ministry effectiveness, Paul doesn't lead with self-defense. He doesn't lead with argument. He doesn't lead with counterattack. He leads with comfort—comfort that he has received from the God of all comfort, and comfort that he desires to extend to them. People in a difficult place and very much in need of remembering where true comfort is found.

But God's comfort doesn't always come in expected ways.

God's Comforting Ways

The story is told of a man who, while walking along distractedly one day, fell into a deep hole from which he could not climb out. Crying for help, he despaired of whether help would ever come. After a while, a doctor came along, and after seeing the man's plight, wrote him a prescription, dropped it down to the man trapped in the hole, and went on his way. After more time had passed, a second person—a religionist—heard the man's pleas. After pondering the situation, the religious man wrote out a prayer for rescue and dropped it into the hole before walking away.

Soon, the man's best friend came. Hearing his friend's shouts, he shockingly jumped into the hole! The trapped man looked at him incredulously and asked, "What are you doing?

Now we're both trapped!" The friend replied, "It's okay. I've been down here before and I know the way out."

Like the good friend that he was, Paul had been where the Corinthians were, and he knew the way out. The way to help. The way to comfort. Repeatedly in 2 Corinthians, Paul describes his own debilitating life experiences—culminating in the shocking list of his sufferings captured in 2 Corinthians 11, ranging from stonings to beatings to shipwreck to imprisonment. The price Paul was paying for carrying the gospel also gave him perspective on the price they were paying for being Christ-followers in a difficult place. This was followed by his explanation of his "thorn in the flesh" in chapter 12, where a messenger of Satan was being allowed to torment him in some way—to keep him from becoming arrogant about everything God was revealing to him.

Paul honestly, candidly, and almost painfully reveals his own times of crushing and loss. In deeply felt words, the apostle combines the struggle of his past with the comfort of God's presence. For example, in 2 Corinthians 4:8–11 we read:

> We are afflicted in every way, but not crushed; perplexed, but not despairing; persecuted, but not forsaken; struck down, but not destroyed; always carrying about in the body the dying of Jesus, so that the life of Jesus also may be manifested in our body. For we who live are constantly being delivered over to death for Jesus' sake, so that the life of Jesus also may be manifested in our mortal flesh.

Paul seeks neither to glorify his suffering nor to minimize it. However, it is really, really, really real. He has lived it. He sees where the Corinthians are and joins them there, for he has been there before. But that isn't all. What Paul describes is the care of the God of all comfort. And the pain and struggle of his own experience anticipates God's surprising response in chapter 7, where we encounter another "but God" we need to consider:

> For even when we came into Macedonia our flesh had no rest, but we were afflicted on every side: conflicts without, fears within. **But God**, who comforts the depressed, comforted us by the coming of Titus; and not only by his coming, but also by the comfort with which he was comforted in you, as he reported to us your longing, your mourning, your zeal for me; so that I rejoiced even more. (2 Corinthians 7:5–7)

There it is—"conflicts without, fears within" (v. 5).

"**But God**, who comforts the depressed, comforted us by the coming of Titus." (v. 6).

Notice the clarity of Paul's remarks. He shares with the Corinthians that God has comforted him greatly, but that this comfort is not limited to him and his personal concerns. The God of all comfort is the one who comforts the depressed. Who is included in that admittedly loaded word?

Strong's Concordance says that the word *depressed* is the Greek word *tapeinos*. What does it mean? Yes, it can mean "depressed," but it can also mean "humiliated . . . base, cast down, humble, of low degree (estate), lowly." It speaks of all of the emotional backwash of the overwhelming fears, dangers, and struggles that could destroy us if left to ourselves. But Paul wants us to be assured that we are *not* left to ourselves. Through Christ, we have access to the God of all comfort. And God uses surprising instruments to deliver that comfort.

But God . . .

Now, it shouldn't be a surprise that God used Titus. This young man was Paul's friend and one of the apostle's protégés. Here, Titus had come to Paul in one of the apostle's darkest seasons and jumped into the hole with him. We all know how God has used those who are significant relationships in our lives to encourage us from time to time.

So, that in itself may not seem overly surprising, but the way God used Titus to provide that comfort is shocking. Titus told Paul of the spiritual progress of his difficult, upsetting, and rebellious friends in Corinth! Paul writes that God, "comforted us by the coming of Titus; and not only by his coming but also by the comfort with which he was comforted in you, as he reported to us your longing, your mourning, your zeal for me; so that I rejoiced even more" (vv. 6–7).

How unexpected! The very people who had been among Paul's greatest causes for concern are now seen as reasons for true joy. Why? Because Titus could relate to the weary apostle. He knew that despite their differences, his affections for the folks at Corinth were not one-sided. They were reciprocal. Now Paul is returning the favor by offering comfort to them in this second letter.

Remember David's "how long" laments in Psalm 13? How many times have we wondered why God didn't intervene in our season of need? How many times have we wondered if He would ever show up? Ever provide help? Ever bring comfort? If we're honest, the answer is likely to be, "Too often." But what if God was working the whole time to bring comfort to us—and we didn't recognize it because it came in unexpected ways and from unexpected places? Paul would not have expected the God of comfort to comfort him through the Corinthians—yet that is how surprising God's ways can be.

A Very Present Help in Time of Trouble

When our little church in the Los Angeles area was on the verge of being evicted—a blow that would have undoubtedly ended that congregation's fragile corporate life—I met with the city officials and was told we had but one recourse. The only path available, other than voluntarily vacating the premises, was to appeal directly to the city council. However, we were also informed in no uncertain terms that in the history of the state, no city council had ever overturned the decision of their building commission.

With no other path available, our landlord provided a real estate attorney and we prepared our appeal, though it all seemed fairly hopeless. The attorney even confirmed that sad fact to me privately. Our church family was praying for a miracle. My own little family was wondering what would happen to us if, having moved across the country to serve this congregation, I was suddenly left without job. Nothing was light. Everything seemed dark.

But God . . .

When we were left without hope, desperately in need of comfort, it happened. The morning of our hearing before the city council, I received a shocking visit from a stranger—an actual member of the building commission that was so determined to close us down. He explained that he had heard about our case and had come to offer his help. Years before, he had helped write the very codes that were now being used as leverage for our removal. He was convinced that those very codes were being misapplied. He asked me to trust him—no small request!—and to come to the council meeting that night ready to agree to what he intended to propose.

As I entered the hall used for public council meetings, almost the entire population of our small church family was quietly seated there, dreading the seemingly inevitable verdict. When our case came up, I spoke on behalf of the congregation, sharing the positive contributions we hoped our ministry efforts could bring to the community. Then the city official who had visited me that morning spoke on our behalf. He presented his view of the misapplication of codes and shared a workable plan that would meet the actual demands of those codes while allowing us to stay in our building. To the shock of everyone there, including the real estate attorney seated beside me, the council voted unanimously to allow us to stay.

Our group left the council meeting and gathered on the steps of the city hall. To an outsider, it may have seemed that our stay of execution was the result of legal hocus pocus or bureaucratic loopholes. But looking into the faces of my brothers and sisters in Christ, I saw in their eyes what I felt profoundly in my heart. The God of all comfort had come to our aid—and He had done so in a way that far surpassed surprise. It was a shock.

But God . . .

God's comfort sometimes comes to us in surprising ways, and we at times surprise others by being conduits of His comfort to them. But it is His comfort that is in play. He is able to come to our aid and comfort our hearts in ways that are, to say the least, unexpected.

John Newton learned this as well. Carrying the burden and guilt of his years as captain of a slaving ship, Newton came to Christ, ultimately entering pastoral ministry. He is now best known as the man who penned the classic hymn "Amazing Grace." In those lyrics, Newton wrote words that must have surprised him and that gave voice to how we felt that night at the city council:

Through many dangers, toils and snares,
I have already come;
'Tis grace hath brought me safe thus far,
And grace will lead me home.

For our little church, the God of surprise had brought us to a home—using a most surprising instrument to get it done. Amazing. Grace.

Comforting Father, I too quickly jump to conclusions about your lack of love and lack of care. I too quickly look for reasons to doubt your comfort instead of trusting you for the surprise of its arrival. Give me grace to trust you more, and remind me that your presence will never fail me—and enable me to be a conduit of your surprising comfort to others.

The Surprising Side of God

And so we end where we began. With the words of the prophet Isaiah, who wrote:

> "For My thoughts are not your thoughts, Nor are your ways My ways," declares the LORD. "For as the heavens are higher than the earth, so are My ways higher than your ways and My thoughts than your thoughts." (Isaiah 55:8–9)

This is true truth—but that doesn't make it easy to accept or trust or believe. Acknowledging the sometimes confusing elements of the wisdom and purposes of God is not the same as actually resting in the wonder of it.

But God . . .

Our God is more than just a distant deity or a mighty sovereign. He is our Father. He calls us His children. He understands that we struggle to understand, and He doesn't throw us away for it. The surprising side of God is that He knows how weak and frail we are and patiently calls us to trust Him. To trust His wisdom. To trust His love. To trust that in all of His perfection He accepts our imperfection and works with the raw materials of our hearts to form Christ there.

His infinite patience is behind everything He does—in our rescue, in giving us life, in using us to accomplish His work, in sticking with us for the long haul, in being our great provision, in showing us His comfort. The God of surprise is also the God who waits so we can learn to walk by faith. So we can learn to live in His love. So we can learn to trust His purposes.

He is the God of surprise—and the God of surprising patience. You can trust Him.

Help us get the word out!

Our Daily Bread Publishing exists to feed the soul with the Word of God.

If you appreciated this book, please let others know.

- Pick up another copy to give as a gift.
- Share a link to the book or mention it on social media.
- Write a review on your blog, on a book-seller's website, or at our own site (ourdailybreadpublishing.org).
- Recommend this book for your church, book club, or small group.

Connect with us:

 @ourdailybread

 @ourdailybread

 @ourdailybread

Our Daily Bread Publishing
PO Box 3566
Grand Rapids, Michigan 49501 USA

 books@odb.org

More from Bill Crowder

Before Christmas

For This He Came

Let's Talk

Living with Courage

Moving Beyond Failure

My Hope Is in You

Overcoming Life's Challenges

Seeing the Heart of Christ

The Spotlight of Faith

Trusting God in Hard Times

Windows on Christmas

Windows on Easter

Available everywhere books are sold.